Growing in Love

FAMILY RESOURCE 6

Part of the love story of salvation

PRINCIPAL PROGRAM CONSULTANTS

James J. DeBoy, Jr., MA
Toinette M. Eugene, PhD
Rev. Richard C. Sparks, CSP, PhD

CONSULTANTS

Sr. Jude Fitzpatrick, CHM
Pedagogy

Rev. Mark A. Ressler
Theology

Rev. Douglas O. Wathier
Theology

Daniel J. Bohle, MD (Obstetrics and Gynecology) and Anne Bohle, RN
Family Medicine and Parenting

REVIEWERS

Sr. Connie Carrigan, SSND
Religion Coordinator
Archdiocese of Miami
Miami, Florida

Mark Ciesielski
Associate Director, Office
of Continuing Christian
Education
Diocese of
Galveston-Houston
Houston, Texas

Margaret Vale DeBoy
Teacher
Arbutus Middle School
Arbutus, Maryland

Diane Dougherty
Director of Children's and
Family Catechesis
Archdiocese of Atlanta
Atlanta, Georgia

Harry J. Dudley, D. Min.
Associate Executive
Director of Faith
Formation
Archdiocese of
Indianapolis
Indianapolis, Indiana

Steven M. Ellair
Diocesan Consultant for
Elementary Catechesis
Archdiocese of Los Angeles
Los Angeles, California

Kirk Gaddy
Principal
St. Katharine Campus/
Queen of Peace School
Baltimore, Maryland

Connie McGhee
Principal
Most Holy Trinity School
San Jose, California

Barbara Minczewski
Religion Formation
Coordinator
Diocese of Davenport
Davenport, Iowa

Sr. Judy O'Brien, IHM
Rockville Centre, New York

Kenneth E. Ortega
Consultant for Media and
Curriculum
Diocese of Joliet
Joliet, Illinois

Sr. Barbara Scully, SUSC
Assistant Director of
Religious Education
Archdiocese of Boston
Randolph, Massachusetts

Rev. John H. West, STD
Theological Consultant,
Department of Education
Archdiocese of Detroit
Rector, St. John's Center for
Youth and Families
Plymouth, Michigan

Our Sunday Visitor

Curriculum Division

Life from Love

Chapter Summary

- God created all things out of love.
- God's gift of life is precious at all its stages.
- Taking care of ourselves as we grow shows respect for God's gift of life.

The Teaching Church

The Gospel of God's love for man, the Gospel of the dignity of the person and the Gospel of life are a single and indivisible Gospel.

The Gospel of Life, #2

All human life is sacred because it is created by God. He sustains all human life; therefore, each person is related to him forever. For this reason, all people are called to protect and preserve human life. No human being has the right to deliberately take the life of an innocent human being, no matter what the circumstances. (See *Catechism of the Catholic Church*, # 2258.) That is why the Church's prohibition of abortion and euthanasia is so strong and consistent.

This consistent ethic of life raises a number of issues, nonetheless. For example, what should a Catholic believe regarding capital punishment or a soldier's conduct in a just war? The Church teaches that, whereas capital punishment might be the only way to preserve the common good in rare circumstances, a government should make every effort possible to find a means of deterrence that preserves the dignity of every human life. Regarding war, governments are obliged to work for peace, to appreciate the seriousness of the choice to go to war, and to avoid it whenever a non-violent solution can be found.

Living the Teaching

The late Joseph Cardinal Bernardin of Chicago referred to the consistent ethic of the sanctity of human life as a "seamless garment." Love of one's neighbor is not a selective activity. Cardinal Bernardin reminds you that all Christians must ask themselves and their government the same basic question: Have I (we) done everything possible in this circumstance to preserve the dignity and holiness of human life?

- In your own thinking, what life-related issues have been the hardest for you to resolve?
- How does your family show concern for society's most vulnerable—the unborn, the disabled, or the elderly?
- When life issues, such as capital punishment, war, abortion, or assisted suicide, are in the news, how do you address them in your home?

Getting Started

Share memories of special gifts you've received and how you cared for them. Consider specific ways you can care for creation, in your home or neighborhood, as you would for a gift.

Talk about actions that show the power and importance of breath, such as blowing up a balloon or giving an injured person mouth-to-mouth resuscitation. What does it mean to you to have God's life and breath in you? How does that affect the choices you make?

Building Understanding

Talk about what it means to treat the body as a gift of God. Have a frank discussion about people who are laughed at because of their looks. Let your child explain why this is wrong.

The Church has a consistent ethic of life.

Comment on the ways you see your child showing self-respect. See what improvements your child feels he or she may need in regard to physical, mental, or spiritual health. Together, work out a plan that can help meet these needs.

Continuing to Grow

Have your child find a few ads that appeal to him or her in a magazine or newspaper. Discuss the ads in relation to the activity on page 10 of your child's book. Do the ads show respect? For whom or for what?

Focus on the photo on page 11 of your child's book. Talk about the signs of long life shown in the person's face. What can younger people learn from those who are elderly? Read the reflection. What does it mean to be "fully alive"?

Together, review Chapter 1 and see whether this raises any additional questions or comments. Initial the HomeLink box on page 10 of your child's book to show that you reviewed the chapter. Add any remarks or questions you may have.

Words from This Chapter

sacred *(p. 6):* Holy; worthy of respect; blessed by God.

abortion *(p. 6):* The death of an unborn baby; *spontaneous abortion*, or *miscarriage*, occurs when the unborn baby dies of natural causes; *direct abortion*, any intentional action taken purposely to cause the death of the unborn baby, is a serious sin.

euthanasia *(p. 7):* Deliberately causing the death of a person who is ill, disabled, or elderly, or assisting such a person to commit suicide.

suicide *(p. 7):* Taking one's own life.

self-respect *(p. 8):* A healthy appreciation of one's own person, including one's strengths and limitations.

temperance *(p. 8):* Moderation; a balance among our wants and needs; a balance between our own wants and needs and those of other people.

When Children Ask

What's wrong with capital punishment? Don't some people deserve to die for the terrible things they've done to others?

Catholics believe that all life comes from God and belongs to him. When a person of sound mind directly or intentionally takes the life of another, he or she commits a grave sin. The government has an obligation to protect the lives of all its citizens. Therefore, it has the right and the obligation to choose a punishment for a murderer that reflects the seriousness of the crime. However, the Catholic Church teaches that capital punishment is almost never a just or necessary solution (See *Catechism of the Catholic Church,* #2266- 7).

The first goal of the punishment is to protect the lives of citizens against the injustice of another person. If any other means of punishment seems just and will make the murderer incapable of doing further harm, such means should be chosen over the taking the murderer's life. Preserving the life of the murderer, however hard it is for citizens or loved ones of the victim to accept, also holds open the possibility of the murderer's conversion of heart and reconciliation with God.

Chapter 2

Covenant of Love

Chapter Summary

- God calls us into a personal relationship.
- One way we learn about God's love is from the Scriptures.
- We live our covenant with God by following the Great Commandment.

The Teaching Church

They shall be my people, and I will be their God . . . . I will make with them an eternal covenant, never to cease doing good to them; into their hearts I will put the fear of me, that they may never depart from me.

Jeremiah 32:38, 40

Many stories in the first five books of the Bible concern the covenant that God made with people of his choosing. A covenant is a binding agreement between parties, through which they enter voluntarily into a long-term, personal relationship. The important difference between God's covenant and merely human covenants is that in the case of God's covenant with humans, he acts first. Through the covenant he established, he showed his willingness to enter into relationship with humanity and to be faithful to his people forever.

A covenant always involves an exchange of promises. Like the marriage relationship, by which a man and a woman establish between themselves a lifetime partnership, God's covenant with his people was designed to bring about a permanent relationship of love. Jesus summed up the duties required of you in the Great Commandment: "You shall love the Lord, your God, with all your heart, with all your being, with all your strength, and with all your mind, and your neighbor as yourself" (Luke 10:27).

Living the Teaching

Living out the covenant with God seems never to have been easy for people. Those who have managed to achieve virtuous lives teach that the secret to living out the covenant is practice. The more you choose what is good and right, the easier the task becomes. And because of the forgiving God most fully revealed by Jesus, it is never too late to begin again.

- How do you respond to your children's mistakes?
- What do your children see you doing to further the cause of justice?
- What opportunities do you give your children to do what is right and good?

Getting Started

Share ideas about the importance of promises. Make a specific promise to spend time together or to help each other. If you wish, put the promise in writing.

Enjoy an activity together that involves doing your best, such as studying for a test or weeding the garden. Share the point that the covenant between people and God requires that people be the best they can be.

Building Understanding

Talk about charity and justice in everyday ways. Besides a handout, what shows charity? How is justice shown at home? In an office or factory? What kind of attitude does charity need?

In addition to honest praise and affirmation, look for ways that you can boost your child's self-esteem. One way is to help your child find an activity he or she feels good about doing.

Relationships are grounded in good communication. Share ideas about the type of communication needed between friends. Discuss whether this would differ for communication between family members or between an individual person and God.

Continuing to Grow

You may want to begin the activity on page 18 of your child's book by talking about some acts of love or justice you have recently noticed. Review the activity with your child once she or he has completed it.

The photo on page 19 of your child's book shows a triceps, a symbol for the Trinity made up of three linked triangles. The triangle shape echoes the flow of love, justice, and peace between God and humans. In prayer, ask God to show you ways to change the earth through promoting peace and justice. Look for possible ways to work for peace and justice this week.

Together, review Chapter 2. Use the photos to help review the text. Initial the HomeLink box on page 18 of your child's book to indicate that you have reviewed the chapter. List any comments or questions you may have.

Words from This Chapter

covenant *(p. 13):* A sacred promise or agreement joining God and humans in relationship.

charity *(p. 15):* The virtue of loving others for their own sake and as an extension and expression of one's love of God.

justice *(p. 15):* The moral virtue expressed in the constant will to give God and others what is due them; fairness.

When Children Ask

There's so much injustice in the world. How can one person, especially somebody like me, make a difference?

Share with your child this well-known quote by Edmund Burke: "The only thing necessary for evil to triumph is for good [people] to do nothing." Tell them that they must not wait for somebody else to make the world a more just or compassionate place. No one person can make it happen; each person must help to make the world a better place. Justice, peace, compassion, and love increase in this world as each person lives out those virtues day by day, treating family, friends, and neighbors justly, compassionately, and with love. This is the way in which the fullness of the reign of God will come in the power of God's grace.

Chapter 3

Christian Love

Chapter Summary

- Christian love finds meaning in the Paschal mystery.
- We live our baptismal commitment in our relationships with God and others.
- Jesus is the fullness of God's revelation.
- Self-sacrifice is part of real love.

The Teaching Church

Like all our human powers and freedoms, sexuality, a gift from God, can be channeled for good or ill. Each of us is entrusted by God with the responsibility to guide and direct this gift wisely and lovingly.

Human Sexuality, 10

Christians are immersed in the death-to-life mystery of Jesus Christ at Baptism. Joined to Christ, you receive God's promise of eternal life. By entering into his Paschal mystery, the mystery of Jesus' suffering, death, Resurrection, and Ascension, you discover the life-giving meaning of Christian love. Just as Jesus was willing to lay down his life for his friends (see John 15:13), Catholics strive to follow his example through self-sacrifice and by doing good for others.

The ability to sacrifice for others results from the practice of self-discipline and the virtues of temperance and generosity. Christian self-sacrifice involves, not punishing yourself or seeking approval, but working generously to secure the good for others. Through self-discipline, you can learn to temper selfish impulses and free yourself to make choices that bring about a greater benefit for all concerned. Self-discipline is a path that leads to wisdom and to holiness.

Living the Teaching

The self-sacrifice of Jesus was a gift given for those he loved. So it should be for his followers. By practicing self-discipline, you learn to give to others as Jesus did. Self-discipline teaches you how to keep your impulses from running (and ruining) your life. Your child will need your example and your encouragement to develop this skill, for the culture in which he or she is living often carries quite a different message.

- When have you sacrificed your own desires for the good of others?
- What impulses do you find hardest to resist?
- What are your children learning from you about the value of self-discipline?

Getting Started

Look for or talk about things in nature that seem to die and come back to life or those that die and give life to something else.

Talk about the command Jesus gives us to love one another. Relate it to the demands of everyday life. When is it easy to follow? When is it challenging?

Building Understanding

You may want to use the image of "walking in another's shoes" when there's a need for empathy and understanding in your home. Your child can draw or find a picture of shoes to display as a reminder to be compassionate to others.

If there's someone your child admires, talk about the possible roles that discipline and self-sacrifice play in that person's life. Share examples of these two habits in your family's life.

Discuss with your child ways to try to be safe from sexual predators. Share the names of "safe" people or places a child could go to for help.

Continuing to Grow

In updating the story of the Good Samaritan (see the activity on page 26 of your child's book), identify the characters who neglected to give help as people who are usually stereotyped as "good." The helpful person chosen should be someone who is usually seen as "no good." What act of compassion did your child choose for the ending?

Look at the photo on page 27 of your child's book, and share the idea that nothing separates us from God's love. Read the reflection. Share a time you felt God's love through the love your child showed you.

Together, review Chapter 3. Initial the HomeLink box on page 26 of your child's book to show that you know what was covered in the chapter. Add any comments or questions that you may have.

Words from This Chapter

compassion *(p. 23):* The quality of love that shares the sufferings of others.

self-sacrifice *(p. 24):* The ability to put aside one's own narrow, limited interests for a greater good or in order to help another.

discipline *(p. 24):* Self-control; moderation; restraint; a learned and practiced strategy for developing character.

sexual abuse *(p. 25):* The mistreatment of another person through improper sexual contact.

When Children Ask
Isn't abstinence unnatural?

Today's culture teaches young people that fulfilling all their desires and wants will bring about happiness. Self-denial is looked upon as unnatural. Tell your child that while the sexual drive is very strong, it is not a biological need, like hunger or thirst, that must be filled. The gratification of sexual intimacy can be postponed or even put off permanently without harmful physical or psychological consequences. Explain that practicing abstinence takes self-discipline, but the results are worth the effort. Mention that sexual activity between couples before marriage has been shown to be a factor in the high incidence of divorce.

Practicing Love

Chapter Summary
- The Church protects and nurtures God's gift of life.
- The Church's magisterium teaches the right use of God's gift of sexuality.
- The Church reaches out to people who feel unloved, lonely, or excluded.

The Teaching Church

Against the pessimism and selfishness which cast a shadow over the world, the Church stands for life: in each human life she sees the splendor of that "Yes," that "Amen," who is Christ himself . . . .

On the Family, #30

The teaching authority of the Catholic Church, the *magisterium*, protects the authentic teaching of Christ against dilution or error. In so doing, the teaching office of the Church makes it possible for you to profess the true faith in its completeness. The Church firmly teaches that human life, even at its weakest and most vulnerable points, is a gift from God, the Author of life. For this reason, the Church stands ready to defend each person against anyone or anything who would harm or diminish the value of human life.

The Church's teaching about human life is at the heart of its teachings about human sexuality and bioethical issues—those issues related to the preservation of human life from conception until death. God's gift of sexuality must never be misused in a way that diminishes or offends the dignity of the human person. That is why the Church's teaching on such issues as adultery, sexual abuse, and incest is so strong. All are grave offenses against the sixth commandment. Bioethics calls upon both individuals and the state to support only those actions that protect and nurture life. The Church's teaching in both these areas shows to the world, with unwavering conviction, its intention to defend the dignity of human life, whatever its condition or state of development, against all attacks that would diminish, degrade, or end it by unnatural means.

Living the Teaching

Sexual and bioethical issues are addressed regularly in the popular media. The Church's teaching often stands against popular opinion. Teach your child what the Church teaches. Point out that the Church's teaching is not illogical or artificially imposed. It is rooted in the natural moral law, the God-given moral sense that helps them tell right from wrong and in divine Revelation.

- How informed are you about bioethical issues—both beginning and end-of-life issues?
- How are you helping your child understand Church teaching on sexuality and bioethical issues?

Pregnancy & Childbirth

One of the fundamental truths of Christianity is that Jesus is the incarnation of God. He is at once fully human and fully divine. This is a great mystery, and it is true. This single fact is the foundation of all we believe about human sexuality.

The annunciation, birth, life, death, and resurrection of Jesus affirm our dignity as humans. These events remind us of how much God loves humanity. It is God's involvement with humanity that makes human reproduction more than a physical act. When a man and woman join together in Christian marriage and choose to have a child, they are participating with God in the creation of a new human person who is both body and spirit. God has graced our humanity in the Person of Jesus, and Jesus reveals that all human life is graced by God.

Talking with Your Child

Parents have the responsibility to hand on to their children the values that have been given to them by their families, their community, and their Church. Any conversation about human sexuality must be placed within the context of Christian morality. That is especially true of the miracle of human conception, pregnancy, and childbirth.

The information in this booklet is provided to you at this time because your sixth grader is approaching or has reached the age of puberty. However, the decision of when to talk to your child about human pregnancy and childbirth belongs completely to you and your spouse. Your decision will be influenced by Church guidance, recommendations by medical, scientific, and other experts and the circumstances of your family life, your child's experience, and your personal preference.

- **Use this information if and when it is helpful** to you in sharing with your child about the unique gift of human pregnancy and childbirth.

- **Respond to your child's questions as honestly as possible.** Understand that questions about pregnancy and childbirth will naturally lead to other questions about sexuality issues. Be prepared to discuss these issues openly with your child and to provide additional information as necessary.

- **Promote respectful attitudes.** Help your child see pregnancy and childbirth as natural parts of God's gift of life that are to be honored as sacred. Don't emphasize the pain of childbirth or dwell on possible complications. If your family is faced with a teen pregnancy or another difficult situation, remind your child that new life is always a gift to be treasured, no matter what the circumstances.

Four Principles

1. Each child is a unique and unrepeatable person and must receive individualized formation. . .
2. The moral dimension must always be a part of their explanations. . .
3. Formation in chastity and timely information regarding sexuality must be provided in the broadest context of education for love. . .
4. Parents should provide this information with great delicacy, but clearly and at the appropriate time. . .

From *The Truth and Meaning of Human Sexuality*, #65–75

The Conception
of *New Life*

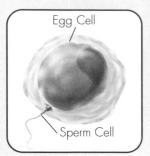

Conception occurs when a sperm cell fertilizes an egg cell.

Sexual intercourse is intended to be a pleasurable act of love and a sign of a husband and wife's total and permanent commitment to each other. It also is the process designed by God by which they can participate in the creation of new life. For these reasons, sexual intercourse is reserved to husbands and wives joined together in marriage.

In the act of intercourse, the husband's penis becomes erect, and he inserts it into the vagina of his wife. At the peak of their lovemaking, the penis emits semen, a white milky fluid that contains sperm cells. If a sperm cell travels into the woman's uterus and **fertilizes**, or joins with, an egg cell, a new human life begins. This moment is called **conception**, which means "beginning." The fertilized egg attaches itself to the lining of the woman's uterus and begins to grow. The woman is now **pregnant**.

The Stages of Pregnancy

A standard pregnancy takes about 280 days, or forty weeks. However, a normal pregnancy can last anywhere from thirty-eight to more than forty-two weeks. The stages of pregnancy are measured in **trimesters**, or thirds.

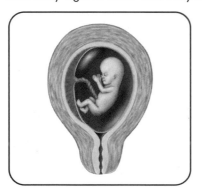

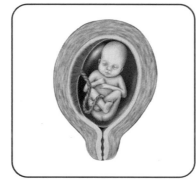

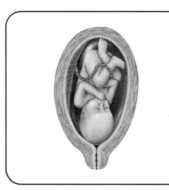

The First Trimester

During the first eight weeks the new life is called an **embryo**, and then a **fetus** from eight weeks until birth. The embryo receives nourishment through the **umbilical cord**. He or she is connected to the wall of the mother's uterus by the **placenta**, a mass of spongy tissue and blood vessels through which the embryo receives nutrition from the mother. During this time the nervous, circulatory, and digestive systems develop. The embryo floats in **amniotic fluid**, within an enclosed sac within the uterus. By the end of the first trimester, the fetus has a large head, and the ears, eyes, nose, and mouth are recognizable. At the end of twelve weeks, the baby is about three inches long.

The Second Trimester

The bones and skeletal system of the fetus develop. The mother's abdomen enlarges as the baby grows. The arms and legs of the fetus grow in proportion to the body. The baby's gender can be determined with an ultrasound scan by twenty weeks. By eighteen to twenty-two weeks, the mother experiences **quickening**, or her first experience of movements of the baby inside the uterus. At twenty-four weeks, the fetus is about thirteen inches long.

The Third Trimester

The brain develops much more. The fetus has a good chance of survival if it is born after twenty-five to twenty-six weeks. By thirty-four weeks, the baby ordinarily moves into a head-down position to prepare for birth. During the final weeks of pregnancy, the baby stores fat and fully develops. It moves lower into the pelvis in preparation for birth at around forty weeks.

The **Process** of *Childbirth*

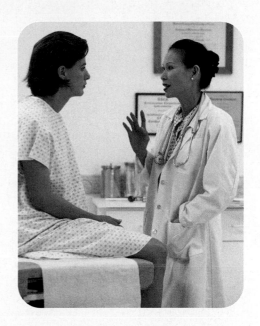

Early in a woman's pregnancy, the doctor tells her when she should expect her baby to be born. The father, the mother, and other family members make plans for the baby's birth. The doctor tells the mother what to expect when it is time for the baby to be born. Often, the father plans to be present as well.

The Three Stages of Labor

The process of giving birth is called **labor**. During labor the muscles of the mother's uterus tighten and contract over and over. The pressure of these **contractions** will help push the baby out of the mother's body. There are three stages to labor.

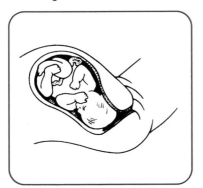 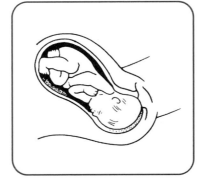 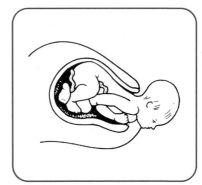

Stage 1
During the first stage of labor, the contractions of the uterus work to expand the opening of the uterus, which is called the **cervix**. Usually, the sac containing the amniotic fluid breaks and fluid comes out of the vagina. When the cervix has expanded enough, the baby begins to emerge from the uterus and its head enters the vagina. This stage of labor may last twelve hours or longer.

Stage 2
When the cervix is fully open, the baby moves farther into the vagina. Once the baby's head comes out of the vagina, the rest of the baby's body slips out easily. Finally, the baby is born. The doctor or other helper then cuts the umbilical cord. This whole process may take only a few minutes or last several hours.

Stage 3
A few minutes after the baby is born, the muscles of the uterus force out the placenta and the rest of the umbilical cord. These are called the **afterbirth**. This ends the third stage of labor.

The newborn baby may let out a cry, which shows that its lungs are working. A nurse or other helper quickly checks the baby's health. Then the mother may hold her baby for the first time. A new human being has been born!

Special Birth Issues

Natural Childbirth

Although labor is hard work and can be very painful for the mother, many women choose to avoid most pain medication by practicing breathing techniques and exercises called **natural childbirth**. The woman's husband or another coach participates in the practice sessions and assists her during the process of labor and childbirth.

If the labor is long or complicated, or if the baby shows signs of physical distress, medications can help relax the mother and can speed up the delivery. In emergencies, or when the health of the mother or baby may be jeopardized by vaginal delivery, a baby can be delivered surgically by cutting into the uterus, in a process known as **caesarean section**.

Breast-Feeding

Humans are mammals, which means mothers are capable of producing special substances to feed their young. In humans the mammary glands in the female breasts produce milk. Milk production, or **lactation**, begins in the late stages of pregnancy. If the mother chooses to breast-feed, the newborn baby is often given the breast in the first minutes after birth. The action of the child sucking at the nipple stimulates the flow of a thin, nutritious liquid called **colostrum**. In a day or two, the colostrum is replaced by breast milk, which contains all the nutrients a baby needs.

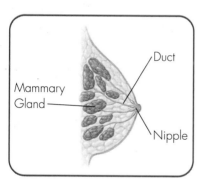

Breast milk is manufactured in the mammary glands and carried to the nipple by a series of ducts.

Breast-feeding supplies more than nutrition. Breast milk is the most easily digested food for babies, and both colostrum and breast milk contain antibodies against many diseases. Babies who are breast-fed for even a short time have less chance of developing food allergies and are less susceptible to germs or infections than babies who are fed formulas.

Breast-feeding has benefits for the mother, too. The action of nursing helps develop an emotional bond between mother and child. Many women find that the pleasurable sensation of nursing stimulates uterine contractions that help the uterus regain muscle tone and return to its normal size after pregnancy. Breast-feeding may inhibit ovulation, providing families with a natural means of spacing pregnancies.

Breast-feeding, or nursing, has health benefits for both mother and child.

It is possible to breast-feed children for several years. This is common practice in parts of the world where infant nutritional needs are difficult to meet. In our society, many children are weaned (switched from breast milk to cow's milk or another substitute) by the sixth month. Mothers who breast-feed longer usually begin introducing the child to other liquids at around three months.

Mothers who do not choose or are unable to breast-feed their babies can provide adequate nutrition by bottle-feeding with substitute formulas based on cow's milk or soy.

Getting Started

Tell about or show your child some fashions you wore when you were younger. Discuss how living the right way is not a matter of style. Share something you learned long ago that helps you lead a Christian life today because it's still true.

With your child, discuss ways that you can work together for the good of your family or for the good of your parish or neighborhood.

Building Understanding

Inspect a piece of cloth so that your child sees how closely the fibers are connected. Compare this to the body of Church teachings. Emphasize that an action does not become wrong because the Church condemns it. The Church condemns an action because it is wrong in itself.

In general terms, discuss the value of abstinence for all who are unmarried, even adults. Recall the importance of discipline and self-sacrifice in relationships. Using specific examples, talk about the possible consequences of acting on sexual and nonsexual impulses.

The Church separates the sin from the sinner. A repentant sinner can be forgiven. Apply this thinking in your own family. Separate the action from the doer. Label an action as "a wrong choice" instead of labeling the person who made the choice.

Continuing to Grow

With your child, review or complete the activity on page 34. Guide your child to give specific, not general, answers. See whether there's someone in your community or parish who may need a healing action.

If you wish, put your arms around each other as you read aloud the reflection on page 35. Give each family member a hug today.

Together, review Chapter 4, using the photos as prompts. See whether new questions or comments arise. Initial the HomeLink box to show that you've seen the chapter. Add any comments or questions that you may have.

Words from This Chapter

magisterium *(p. 28):* The teaching authority of the Church, given by Christ through the Holy Spirit and found in the bishops in union with the pope.

bioethics *(p. 28):* The moral values associated with choices and actions regarding medicine, health care, and research on human life.

natural moral law *(p. 29):* The moral sense that allows humans to distinguish right from wrong by the use of reason; natural moral law is universal and transcends cultural differences.

abstinence *(p. 31):* Avoiding a particular behavior, such as the genital expression of sexuality.

HIV *(p. 33):* Human immunodeficiency virus, a blood-borne infection transmitted through sexual contact, the sharing of intravenous drug needles, or the transfusion of infected blood, or passed from infected mothers to unborn children.

AIDS *(p. 33):* Acquired immune deficiency syndrome, a weakening of the immune system caused by infection with HIV; AIDS leaves the body subject to a number of serious, potentially fatal diseases.

When Children Ask

What is AIDS? How do people get it?

The issue of AIDS—Acquired Immune Deficiency Syndrome—is related both to the Catholic Church's sexuality teaching and to bioethical issues. AIDS is a complex of symptoms associated with infection by HIV (human immunodeficiency virus). HIV attacks the body's immune system, leaving it vulnerable to a number of serious and potentially fatal infections and diseases. The virus that causes AIDS is carried in the bloodstream and spread through direct contact with blood, semen, and other body fluids. HIV is commonly transmitted by (1) sexual contact with an infected person, (2) injection by contaminated needles, (3) transference from an infected mother to a child—in the womb, during birth, or through breastfeeding, (4) transfusion from infected blood, and (5) use of unsterilized medical or dental instruments. Because one cause of AIDS is high-risk sexual behavior, the Church's teaching on reserving sexual intercourse for marriage promotes protection against AIDS and other STDs (sexually transmitted diseases). The Church's fundamental teaching on the dignity of every human person requires all to show compassion and care toward all persons who have this serious illness.

Chapter 5

Holy and Whole

Chapter Summary

- God's grace is given to us as a gift.
- Humans are attracted to some things that can be sinful.
- The Holy Spirit guides us in living our call to holiness and wholeness.

The Teaching Church

Each of us is called to be sexually responsible and chaste in whatever vocation we discern. God's grace is sufficient for us, if we are open and responsive to it.

Human Sexuality, 27

The Catholic Church recognizes that the process of becoming humanly whole and holy is difficult. The process involves mastering the passions and controlling impulses, but this is the path to inner peace. Either a person governs the passions and finds peace or is a person dominated by them and becomes unhappy.

Becoming whole and holy is especially challenging in today's world, where many habits of speech and conduct trivialize sexuality and undermine the search for the integration of body and spirit. With the help of the Holy Spirit, Christian parents can help their children learn to resist those habits and influences. You can help your child temper these influences with the virtues of chastity, modesty, and moderation that are characteristic of a truly integrated personality.

Living the Teaching

The practice of chastity is a key to self-mastery. Chastity is based in self-control. It is related to the virtue of temperance, which seeks to bring the passions and the sense appetites under the control of reason. Both virtues assist in developing the balance between body and spirit that characterize a person who is both holy and whole. Virtues are lived day-by-day. They take practice until, eventually, they become habits of life.

- What level of self-mastery and self-control have you attained?
- How do you deal with temptation?
- What is your child learning from you about avoiding temptation?

Getting Started

Talk about a time you felt God's presence in your life. Ask your child to mention some people or things that could tempt him or her to turn away from God. How are these situations handled?

With your child, discuss these questions: Do you really believe that God created you with weaknesses and strengths? How can a weakness be a strength?

Building Understanding

Review the various relationships your child has. Let your child tell the proper, respectful behavior that is appropriate in each relationship.

Be sure your child knows that temptations and attractions are normal and natural. They are not wrong. What could be wrong is the way a person chooses to respond to them. Give a few examples of realistic temptations, and talk with your child about the ways each could be handled and why.

Toss a pebble into a sink full of water and watch the rippling effect. Help your child understand that our choices have many effects, too. The person making the choice is responsible. You might find an example from the nightly news that ties in.

Continuing to Grow

Discuss with your child the exercise on page 42 of his or her book. Encourage honesty in the responses. You may wish to share a risk you are often tempted to take.

Light a candle or stand in a sunny space when you read aloud the reflection on page 43. Then, in your own words, say a quiet prayer to the Holy Spirit for help in staying close to God.

Together, review Chapter 5. See whether there are any other points to talk about. Initial the HomeLink box to indicate that you have reviewed the chapter. If you wish, add a comment or question.

Words from This Chapter

grace *(p. 36):* God's life in us, freely given; loving relationship with God; the free and undeserved help God gives us to respond to the call to holiness.

concupiscence *(p. 38):* The tendency or inclination to choose what is wrong that is part of our weakened human nature as the effect of original sin.

lust *(p. 38):* The excessive desire for sexual pleasure unrelated to love and commitment.

masturbation *(p. 39):* The deliberate self-stimulation of the genitals solely for one's own sexual pleasure.

When Children Ask

What's wrong with masturbation?

Tell your child that masturbation (deliberately touching the genitals to cause sexual excitement, often leading to orgasm) is a misuse of God's gift of sexuality. It separates sexual pleasure from its true place within the loving relationship between a husband and wife. While it does not cause physical harm, deliberate masturbation is sinful to a greater or lesser degree depending on a person's age, emotional maturity, and other circumstances. Tell your child that if he or she is struggling with sexual feelings and the urge to masturbate, he or she need not be embarrassed. The onset of sexual feeling is normal. It is the choice of masturbation as a response to that feeling that is inappropriate. Talk with your child about ways to channel sexual feelings into more positive activities. Tell your child that if anyone asks him or her to engage in masturbatory activities, he or she should tell you or another family member or trusted adult immediately. Tell your child that it is wrong for someone his or her age to suggest such behavior, and it is sexual abuse for an adult to do so.

Chapter 6

Celebrating **Life**

Chapter Summary

- The Christian family celebrates birth.
- The Anointing of the Sick is a sacrament of God's healing love.
- The Christian family honors the mystery of suffering and death.

The Teaching Church

The seven sacraments touch all the stages and all the important moments of Christian life: they give birth and increase, healing and mission to the Christian's life of faith.

Catechism of the Catholic Church, #1210

The Catholic Church's sacraments celebrate the holiness of life's most significant and mystery-filled events: birth, vocation, conversion, sickness, and death. Because there is a certain resemblance between the stages of natural life and the stages of the spiritual life, the sacraments always seem to be there when you most need their strengthening power.

The Anointing of the Sick, for example, furthers your immersion into the death and Resurrection of Christ, just as surely as Baptism began it. It recalls and completes all the holy anointings that are part of Christian life—from Baptism's anointing, which sealed God's new life in us, to that of Confirmation, which strengthened us for life's combat. The final Anointing of the Sick fortifies us as we face the struggle that ends our earthly life, even as it prepares us to fully enter eternal life.

Living the Teaching

The sacraments remind you that God is always with you, through all stages of life, giving you all that you need to respond to his call to holiness. The mystery of sickness and death is particularly hard for young people to understand. The youth culture that surrounds Americans can make them uncomfortable in the presence of those who are elderly, particularly those who are not well or whose faculties are diminishing. Model an appropriately patient and loving attitude yourself toward those who are sick and elderly. If possible, offer your child the opportunity to visit those who are elderly and those with non-contagious illnesses. Attend communal celebrations of the Anointing of the Sick in your parish, and develop the habit of praying for those who are sick and elderly within your home.

- How are you helping your child learn to cope with the mysteries of life and death?
- How do you confront your own aging and issues of physical and emotional health?

Getting Started

Share with your child that life begins at conception. Together, look in an encyclopedia under reproduction, embryo, pregnancy, and birth for photos that show the wonder of human life before birth.

Emphasizing the positive, share the emotions you felt and the preparations you made while waiting for your child's birth or adoption. Tell how you shared the good news with others. Let your child ask you questions about that time.

Building Understanding

Use this opportunity to discuss the challenges your family has experienced and the emotions you have felt when dealing with aging, illness, or death. What help did you want? What did people do to comfort you?

It's natural for a child to be curious about death. Share the ethnic or traditional ways your family ritualizes death and cares for the bereaved. Show your child a prayer card, Mass card, or some other form of remembrance used at a funeral.

"Put on the shoes" of someone you know who is dying or dealing with limitations caused by aging or illness. Imagine some difficult parts of that person's typical day. Pray for strength and peace for those people in your neighborhood or parish who are dying.

Continuing to Grow

It's comforting to know that God is with us in happy times and in sad times. Encourage your child to do the activity on page 50, or help him or her complete the activity.

Spend a few quiet moments feeling God's presence. Pray the reflection together. Then, put your hand on your child's head and ask God to bless your child. Let him or her bless you, too.

With your child, review Chapter 6. Use the photos to help you review the ideas. Initial the HomeLink box to show that you reviewed the chapter. List any questions or comments.

Words from This Chapter

pregnancy *(p. 44):* The nine-month period during which the unborn baby develops in its mother's uterus.

embryo *(p. 44):* The technical name for the unborn baby in its early stages of growth and development.

fetus *(p. 44):* The technical name for the unborn baby from about the third month in the uterus until its birth; the word *fetus* means "young one."

childbirth *(p. 45):* The process by which a child is born; childbirth may occur naturally through the vagina, or *birth canal,* or may be accomplished through abdominal surgery known as a *cesarean section;* other terms for childbirth include *delivery* and *parturition.*

Anointing of the Sick *(p. 49):* The sacrament that celebrates God's healing power for those who are ill, elderly, or at medical risk.

funeral *(p. 49):* The general term for the religious or civil service to honor a person and celebrate his or her life, which is conducted after the person has died.

cremation *(p. 49):* Reducing the body of a deceased person to ashes before interment.

burial *(p. 49):* Placing the body (or ashes, if the body has been cremated) of a deceased person in a grave; also called *interment.*

When Children Ask

Is it true that Catholics cannot be cremated?

Tell your child that many Catholics today still believe that the Church forbids cremation. Prior to the Second Vatican Council (1962–1965), the Church did not permit cremation, except when grave public need required rapid disposition of bodies, as in times of plague or natural disaster. The Church took this position because of its belief in the resurrection of the body and its strong reverence for the body as a member of Christ's body and a temple of the Holy Spirit. From a practical standpoint, many people could not understand how a cremated body could be resurrected. After Vatican Council II, however, the Church began to take into account a greater scientific understanding of the various forms matter can take. It revised its position and no longer forbids cremation. However, the Church still strongly recommends that the remains of Catholics be buried in a Catholic cemetery, for that serves as a visible sign of the faith community. Christian burial attests to the dignity of baptized persons and to the promise of the resurrection of the body.

Love in Action

Chapter Summary

- The Beatitudes show us how Jesus wants us to love.
- Every Christian has a prophetic mission.
- When the kingdom of God comes in its fullness, our growing in love will be complete.

OSCAR ROMERO DE EL SALVADOR

The Teaching Church

We are all children of God and share in the Lord's call to justice and peace. We cannot call ourselves Catholic unless we hear and heed the Church's teaching to serve those in need, to protect human life and dignity, and to pursue justice and peace.

Sharing Catholic Social Teaching, 22

Jesus' Beatitudes point to the kind of living it takes to be truly happy—service to those in need, those who are poor, and those who suffer. However, in a society characterized by individualism and selfishness, living for others is not seen as the way to happiness. Therefore, it falls on Christian parents to inspire in their children a sense of justice, which leads to respect for the personal dignity of each individual and to furthering God's kingdom on earth.

Insofar as the Christian family is a "small-scale Church," it is called upon, like the "large-scale Church," to be a sign of unity for the world and to bear witness to Christ's kingdom of peace and love, to which the whole world is called. In this way Christian families have a role in helping to further God's kingdom.

Living the Teaching

The Christian family, in its role as witness to Christ's kingdom of peace and love, is called upon to show a preferential option for those who are poor and disadvantaged. The family does so by actively demonstrating special concern for those who are hungry, poor, aged, sick, or unloved.

- How do you show a preferential option for those who are poor and disadvantaged?
- How are you helping your child learn to live the Beatitudes?

Getting Started

Together, look through magazine ads to see what they claim brings happiness. Ask your child whether it's possible for a person to own everything she or he wants and still not be happy. Why is this so?

Look at pages 52–53 of your child's book, and see which of the large-type Beatitudes your child wants to talk about. Choose one of the suggested ways to live this Beatitude, and together make a plan to carry it through.

Building Understanding

Preteens are developing great loyalties to their friends. This can make being a prophet a real challenge. Share an experience of trying to speak or act on God's message of justice, love, or peace in a difficult situation with a friend.

Visit a library or bookstore. Have your child choose a book about a person who has dared to do good in the world. Read it together.

After reading the *Stepping Stones* feature on page 57 of your child's book, talk together about the abilities your child can use to help others, perhaps a sibling or a neighbor. Let your child choose an action, from the list or not, that he or she feels comfortable doing.

Continuing to Grow

The activity on page 58 of your child's book should be done with a sense of importance. Take time to think about the pledge; it needn't be completed at one sitting. Give positive feedback on the decisions your child listed. You may wish to write your own pledge, too.

Look at the photo on page 59 of your child's book, hold hands, and read the Scripture verse. Copy the pledges that were written on page 58, and post them where they can serve as reminders. In a few days, talk about the ways you carried out some of the actions you pledged to do.

Review Chapter 7, and then initial the HomeLink box. Add any questions or comments you may have.

Words from This Chapter

beatitude *(p. 52):* Blessedness; the true happiness for which God created humans.

prophetic *(p. 55):* Communicating God's message of justice, love, and peace in words and actions; the word *prophet* means "one who speaks for another."

solidarity *(p. 57):* The principle of oneness in the family of God; belonging to and being responsible for one another.

When Children Ask

What is civil disobedience? Isn't it wrong to break the law?

Civil disobedience involves refusing to obey specific civil laws or decrees. This refusal usually takes the form of nonviolent or passive resistance. People practicing civil disobedience break a law because they believe that the law is unjust, want to call attention to its injustice, and hope to bring about its repeal or amendment. They believe that they are responding to a higher moral law that requires them to pursue what is true and good, as Jesus did when he cured on the Sabbath, thereby apparently violating the Jewish law to rest on the Lord's Day. A Catholic who chooses to engage in civil disobedience must never engage in a violent act in support of a cause he or she believes is just. Also, men and women who practice civil disobedience must be willing to accept any penalty, including imprisonment, for breaking the law. Choosing to violate a law is a serious decision that should only be undertaken by a mature person after study, reflection, and prayer.

Additional References

These resources may help you answer further questions and continue to talk with your child about sexuality and Catholic values. Some resources listed below are rooted in other Christian traditions and will need to be adapted for Catholic families or supplemented with specifically Catholic teaching.

Before You Were Born, by Henry O'Brien and Joan Lowery Nixon (Our Sunday Visitor, 1980).
    A beautifully illustrated reflection on the miracle of pregnancy and birth, simple enough for young children but useful for all ages. (K–3)
Catholic Sexual Ethics, by Ronald Lawler, Joseph Boyle Jr., and William E. May (Our Sunday Visitor, 1998).
    A sourcebook on Catholic teaching about sexuality issues. (Adult)
Contemporary Christian Morality, by Richard C. Sparks (Crossroad Publishing, 1996).
    One hundred of the most frequently asked questions regarding moral issues answered from a Christian viewpoint. (Adult)
How and When to Tell Your Kids About Sex: A Lifelong Approach to Shaping Your Child's Sexual Character, by Stanton L. Jones and Brenna B. Jones (Navarre Press, 1993).
    This guide comes from an evangelical Christian point of view and does not provide the nuances of Catholic teaching, but it offers parents of all Christian backgrounds a practical and positive approach. (Adult)
How to Talk Confidently with Your Child About Sex . . . And Appreciate Your Own Sexuality, Too, by Lenore Buth (Concordia Publishing House, 1995).
    Practical advice from a Christian perspective. (Adult)
How You Were Born, by Joanna Cole (Morrow Junior Books, 1993).
    An exploration of the beautiful process of childbirth. (K–3)
Know Your Body: A Family Guide to Sexuality and Fertility, by Charles Norris and Jean Weibel Owen (Our Sunday Visitor, 1982).
    Written from a faithful Catholic perspective, this guide is particularly helpful for discussing Natural Family Planning. (Adult)
Sex Education for Toddlers to Young Adults, by James Kenny (St. Anthony Messenger Press, 1989).
    A straight-talking guide for parents regarding many pertinent topics. (Adult)
Sex Is Not a Four-Letter Word! by Patricia Martens Miller (Crossroad Publishing, 1994).
    Practical suggestions for age-appropriate discussions between parents and children regarding sex. (Adult)
Sex Is More than a Plumbing Lesson, by Patty Stark (Preston Hollow Enterprises, 1991).
    Encourages parents to share their values and beliefs regarding sexuality with their own children in age-appropriate ways. (Adult)
Tender Love: God's Gift of Sexual Intimacy, by Bill Hybels and Rob Wilkins (Moody Press, 1993).
    A look at the spiritual side of sexuality and commitment in marriage as necessary to love in a fully human way. (Adult)

Our Sunday Visitor Curriculum Division Multimedia Resources

Catholic Values and Sexuality (video).
    Sixteen significant topics covered through drama and documentary; Parent Guide available. (Jr. High–Adult)
God's Gift (video) (produced by the Archdiocese of St. Paul-Minneapolis).
    Six videos on sexuality topics, geared to children's level of understanding. (K–6)
Growing in Love (video).
    Explores program themes and gives parents background in sharing this material with their children. (Adult)
Marriage (video) (produced by Golden Dome Productions).
    Four videos explore all stages and aspects of married life. (High School–Adult)

Movie and Video Reviews
For ratings and reviews of current and previously released films, go online to **www.usccb.org/movies**. This site, sponsored by the United States Conference of Catholic Bishops' Office for Film and Broadcasting, also features previews of movies and shows coming up on television, reviews of newly released DVDs, archived movies reviews, top 10 movie lists starting from 1965, and the Vatican top 45 movie list.

Photography Credits
Gene Plaisted/The Crosiers: 8, 12; **Digital Imaging Group:** 4, 7, 9, 17; **Susie Fitzhugh:** 13; **Jack Holtel:** 6, 10; **Natural Bridges:** Robert Lentz: 16; **Superstock:** 14; **Tony Stone Images:** David Madison: 5, Bruce Ayres: A-4

Cover
Photo by **Jack Holtel**
Illustration by **Francis Livingston**

Part of the love story
of salvation

"For creation
awaits with eager
anticipation the
revelation of the
children of God."

(Romans 8:19)

OurSundayVisitor

Curriculum Division

www.osvcurriculum.com

Item Number: CU0555
ISBN: 978-0-15901-429-5

9 780159 014295

90000 >